for
Alice
and
Jim...
who will
find their
own family
and
friends
within
these pages

Rae Turnbull
2012

Rae Turnbull

When *Wildflowers are in Bloom*

Publisher
Friend of the Family Features

Design and illustrations by George Turnbull

Published by
Friend of the Family Features
Route 2, Box 2665
Orland, California 95963

Dedicated to my parents,
Philly and Vince Prudente,
who gave me a life
of love and loyalty.

C O N T E N T S

I've never seen her face
or touched her hand,
        but I'm certain,
  by her letters,
      she's my friend.

Distance dims
the opportunity
for us to ever meet,
for it was just by chance
our correspondence
first began.

Since then, we've written
several times,
and by the way
that she responds,
I know whatever I may write,
she will understand.

Our relationship reminds me
how powerful are words,
that they can let us
be such friends,
though I've never
seen her face
or touched her hand.

1

I turned on my old radio,
        and sang right along
    with a favorite song,
        not caring
            if I was in tune.

So good was my mood
I danced round the room,
not minding at all
that my steps were not
graceful and light.

For I learned long ago
to savor the days
when everything's right
with my world.

Then when a sorrow
steals into my soul,
I bear it much better
if I can remember
when I had the chance,
I sang and I danced.

On warm summer nights,
I'd open the windows
in my grandmother's rooms
above her grocery store.

I stayed with her often
when I was young,
and after my work
in the store was done,
I could go read upstairs.

The store's neon light
outside her window
cast a warm glow
on the over-stuffed chair
in her living room.

I loved sitting there,
just reading and listening
to the sounds
from the street.

Perhaps that's the reason
whenever I drive
through a little old town,
and see a neon sign
above a small store,
I look up at the windows
and sometimes I see
that summer reflection
of the child that was me.

3

Mrs. Nesbitt gave us
   homemade cookies every Halloween,
        but even better than the cookies
   was her open admiration.

Eager and excited,
we'd holler trick or treat
at her front door.

She'd greet us with a welcome smile,
and usher us inside.
Before we got our treat,
we paraded in our costumes
for her warm appreciation.

She'd play a gentle game
of guessing who we were.
What fun we had
because we thought
we fooled her.

We all grew up
and moved away,
but Mrs. Nesbitt stayed,
and baked her cookies
every Halloween.

She had no children of her own,
and what a shame.
She knew so well
how to enjoy
a childhood celebration.

When we traveled,
        we took the children with us.
Ever since the youngest was a toddler,
            we took our trips together,
        as a family.

                When friends asked us
                why we always took our children,
                we answered,
                "We'll enjoy them while we can."

                As we traveled,
                I would wonder
                how much of what we shared
                the children would recall.

                Then last year,
                traveling on his own,
                my son stopped at a campground
                we'd been in together,
                when he was just a child.

                "It's changed some," he smiled softly,
                "but the berry bushes are still there."
                I remembered how he and his sister
                picked and ate the berries,
                sweet and wild.

                How glad I am
                that when we traveled,
                we took the children with us.

When I first left home,
I noticed that it didn't matter
how many of us might drop by
for sunday supper,
there was always plenty
on my mother's table.

It was a warm and welcome
feeling,
to know that in
my mother's home,
I always had a place.

When I asked her
how she knew
that we were coming,
she told us
that she made a little extra,
just in case.

Now most of mine are on
their own,
But when I plan
my sunday supper,
I cook for more than two.

I tell myself leftovers
never really go to waste.
Who do I think I'm fooling?
I make a little extra,
just in case.

The man and dog were old.
        Silently, they stood beside
their ancient pick-up truck.
        They were waiting in the parking lot
for someone.

                        The man was bent and stiff,
                        and as he stroked
                        the dog's gray head,
                        the dog's tail made
                        a feeble little motion.

                        Then the market doors burst open,
                        and a small boy came out running
                        toward their truck.

                        I watched the transformation,
                        as the old man straightened up.
                        Laughing now,
                        he scooped the child up in his arms,
                        and got a healthy hug.
                        The old dog, eager for his turn,
                        jumped and barked
                        and briskly wagged his tail.

                        When all three
                        climbed into the cab,
                        I watched them drive away,
                        delighting in the difference
                        made in one old man
                        and one old dog
                        by one small boy.

I was shopping for a gift
        for a brand new mother.
    But I passed by
the baby blankets
        and ignored the tiny clothes.

I wasn't sure
what I was searching for
until I saw the books.

On a shelf, all neatly stacked,
were books of numbers
and nursery rhymes
and ABC's.
Before my children started school,
I read to them
from books like these.

Now as I turn bright colored pages,
I remember eager faces
close to mine.

The blankets might be better,
and a bit more practical,
but I bought the books
and wrapped them as my gift.

I wanted her
to have the chance
for memories like mine.

No one can be certain
  of how they'll be remembered.
      Its not always
  for our grandest schemes
      or any great achievements.

When I picture my Dad's mother,
I seldom see
the strong-willed matriarch
she took such pride in being.

Instead, I see her in a housedress,
dancing to Italian folk songs,
arms held high
and fingers snapping,
while we watched
and clapped our hands.

In light of all the work she did,
she wouldn't think that moment
would be worth remembering.

But it's those unplanned moments,
the little slice of self revealed,
that keep us dancing,
like my Grandma,
in someone's memory.

Let me live my life
right to the end,
surrounded by the things
I have collected through the years,
though most of them have value
just to me.

I know that age may slow me down,
and you will want to help.
You'll ask to clear my closets
and close up extra rooms,
or move me somewhere
that is easy to maintain.

But that will only hurt, not help me.
I don't regard it as a chore
to care for my collected things.
And rooms unused
are really very easy to keep clean.

Though you have good intentions,
if you take away those things
that are a part
of all my years,
and trade them
for some vague security,
you also take away
part of my sense of me.

John Henry doesn't walk,
    he strolls.

Sealpoint Siamese,
his manner is regal,
befitting a descendant
of the courts of kings.

Even as he sits,
he poses,
looking sculptured and serene.
Unhurried,
his blue-eyed gaze
observes all.

A true aristocrat,
he is even graceful
in his few demands,
placing a gentle paw
upon my knee
to tell me that my service
is required.

And I gladly serve him.
For in the shrill
and hurried clamor
of the modern world,
it's nice
to have a little cat
that strolls.

11

There's just a handful of them,
Miss McFarland,
teacher's names I still remember.

I guess they were the ones
who mattered most.
Like you,
the first one who
encouraged me to teach.

I thought you were so wrong,
because I couldn't see myself
as a teacher.
But your words were welcome.

The interest and the confidence
you showed in me,
was exactly what
this unsure young girl needed.
Though it took a lot of time
before I finally realized
how right you were.

The age that I am now,
 you were then,
so I know you may be gone.
And how I wish it were not so.

For I would like to tell you,
Miss McFarland,
that even after all these years,
yours is a teacher's name
I still remember.

Are you sad, son?
  For just a moment,
do I see a look of sadness
    in your eyes?

> We both realize
> that you'll be gone awhile,
> and it was your decision.
>
> You were eager
> to be on your way,
> and that is as it should be.
> There are no regrets
> on either side.
>
> It's simply that I'll miss you,
> and all the times we had
> before
> that, I know,
> are going with you.
>
> So I just wondered,
> for a moment,
> if you felt a little sad.
> Or am I the only one
> who wants to cry?

She offered me some coffee,
and I welcomed it
as though she offered gold.

It could just as easily
have been milk or tea.
The important thing to me
was that she offered.

For somehow, somewhere
along the line,
we had pulled apart.
A friendship once strong
had withered
and lost its heart.

What either of us
did or said
to separate us so,
neither of us
seemed to know.

Yet it remained
until the wiser of us
saw that it must change,
and offered friendship's hand,
holding a cup of coffee.

She sat on the bed,
        sunlight touching
    the top of her head,
            while she looked through
        a magazine.

I watched her,
as we talked
about this thing or that,
her mind not really
on the pages
or the conversation.

Then I settled back,
and let that picture of her
etch itself into my memory . . .
where I could keep it
for the times
when she'd be gone.

For though she hadn't
said a word about it,
I knew her visit
would soon end.

I could sense
that she was
restless to return.
And already,
in her mind,
she was heading home.

*She said she had
     never married
   because she wouldn't
        "settle"
for just anyone.*

That may sound as though
she held herself
above the rest.
Not so at all.

She simply saw
the marriage vows
as a sacred sort
of willing compromise.
And she had yet to find
someone that she felt
inclined
to make adjustments for.

"Better to go
my way alone,"
she always said,
"Than to be untrue
to what a marriage
ought to be . . .
and settle."

We stopped to put
some flowers
on his mother's grave.

And as we walked along the path,
we were solemn,
but we were not sad.

She's been away awhile now,
and in his heart,
there is acceptance.

But as we walked back to the car,
I looked up
at my husband,
and in that moment,
saw my son.

I realized someday
my son must also find
that same acceptance.

I thought of every mother
who had gone before,
and the mothers
yet to come,
and felt a sudden sorrow
for the solemn walks
of every mother's son.

Carnations

Two pink carnations
with soft green ferns
brighten my dining room.

They came as companions
to a tall slender rose
that since has wilted away.
But the pink carnations
still seem fresh,
and their peppermint scent
is still in the air.

Not as grand
or as glorious as the rose,
yet if I must choose
one favorite flower,
the crisp carnation
is what it would be.

It's like a friendship
you take for granted
when brighter
and showier blooms
come around.

But when roses have
withered
and worn out their welcome,
the quiet carnation's
still there.

19

It seemed to be
    the usual garage sale . . .
a collection of things
    no longer wanted.

Each of us
who wandered through
hoped to find a bargain
in what was gathered there.

Then I noticed an old woman
watching from the window.
I was told that she
was once the lady of the house.

Now left alone,
she was moving to
a smaller place,
where there would be
too little space
to keep what she had saved.

As strangers sifted through
a lifetime's legacy,
I saw the sadness on her face.

It was a price
that I was not prepared to pay.
Quietly, I turned
and walked away.

One of my childhood memories
        is of my mother's brother Joe,
    down on his knees,
        arranging the
            little Lionel train set
        under the Christmas tree.

A strapping young man
in his twenties then,
with no family yet
of his own,
he came often to our home . . .
bringing hearty hugs
and easy laughter.

When he married
and moved far away,
we children missed him so.
Especially at Christmas,
the holiday that suited best
his warm and giving ways.

Funny, how one incident
can keep someone forever
in our hearts and minds.
For to this day,
one of my nicest memories
of childhood Christmastimes,
is of a little Lionel train set,
and my mother's brother Joe.

E*ven as a child,*
        he understood commitment.

He took each promise
that he made
quite seriously,
and never made one
he did not
intend to fully keep.

If ever they were broken,
it only was because
he still was learning
what his limits were.

I loved that in him
as a child,
and prize it even more
now that my son is grown.

*All through grade school
and junior high,
everyday, Alice and I
walked all the way home
up Penn Avenue hill.*

The walk was long
and in the winter, quite cold,
but we didn't mind.
We talked the whole way
and the time flew by.

Her house was the first we came to,
with mine just a few doors away.
And sometimes,
if we hadn't quite figured out
what the world was about,
we'd walk back and forth,
between her house and mine,
till we said all we wanted to say.

We laughed and we cried, Alice and I,
as best friends do
in their growing up years.
And it warms my heart still
just to remember
those long, long walks
up Penn Avenue hill.

Well, my friend,
another anniversary
has caught up
with you and me.

By now, we've been together
many more years
than we've been apart.

So many memories,
good and bad,
happy and sad,
crowded into
all of those years.
Memories that weave
our lives into one
well weathered fabric . . .
sturdy yet supple,
like the strongest cotton
and the finest silk.

But that's the way
durable marriages are made . . .
strand by strand,
day by day,
making memories
meant to be saved.

She was saying her goodbyes,
and this time,
she put his off
till the very last.

As she gently stroked the fur
on the big dog's head,
I remembered when
they both were young,
and always side by side.

Then she grew up
and moved away,
much too far
for an old dog to follow.

Now with each visit home,
she sees his signs of age,
and knows too well
there'll come a day
he won't be there
when she arrives.

He has no way of knowing
time takes all of us away.
So he doesn't understand
why she softly cries,
and saves his goodbye
till the last.

Once a week
she took the streetcar from town,
then walked a mile
to our small apartment.

She arrived at my door
just after breakfast,
and stayed till supper time.
She called it my personal day.

All that first year
of my first-born's life,
she gave me that gift of time.

While I dressed up
and spent the day in town,
she tended to all
my household chores,
and tended her first grandchild.

When I tried to thank her
for what she did,
she told me there was no need.

She said we'd both have forever
the memories made
when we shared my son,
and each of us gave the other
a gift of time.

*Barbara's learning the piano
at eighty years of age.
It's a tribute to a friend.*

Close friends for years,
Barbara and Betty
used to sing together.
Betty was the one
who played piano,
while they sang
their favorite songs.

But even friends
who've been together
their whole life long,
must separate one day.
And just last year,
Betty passed away.

Before she did,
she gave Barbara her piano.
Though she knew
Barbara couldn't play it,
she also must have known
Barbara was not one
to let their music end.

They knew each other well,
these two old friends.
Barbara's learning the piano
at eighty years of age.

I stepped into his kitchen,
  and met his memories.

The refrigerator door
was crowded with snapshots
of small children,
now grown and on their own.
And a smiling wife,
before she lost her fight
with illness and with time.

I wandered through
the almost empty rooms,
once filled with family.
Now everything was orderly and neat,
like the sets of baby shoes
bronzed upon the mantlepiece.

Though he lives
in this rambling house alone,
he ignores advice to sell
and find some smaller space.

Why should he go?
To him, this is much more
than just a place.
This is where he made his memories.
This is his home.

She believed that mothering
was in the heart and mind.
And her children
all grew up to be
decent and honest and kind.

No one who knew
of their sturdy upbringing
was ever surprised.
Somehow she channeled
each child's energy
into productive ways.
And somehow she managed
to teach them the rules
without stealing their spirit away.

Unknowing people said
the children inherited
all of her good traits,
and that's what
made them worthwhile.

That always made her smile.
For each of her daughters
and each of her sons
was an adopted child.

She always had
something better to do
when I'd ask her
to clean her room.

Things like riding her bike
to the park,
or walking with the dog
through the wildflowers on the hill.

"I'll get to it soon,"
she'd promise,
when I'd once again
mention her room.

And she did get to it eventually,
though it frustrated me at the time.

But lately I see the value
in her lighthearted point of view.

A child's bicycle
is soon outgrown,
dogs quickly grow old,
and it's such a short time
when wildflowers are in bloom.

My brother writes music.
I express my thoughts with words,
but my brother writes music.

He composes,
moving small white keys
with just his fingertips
to translate
all the singing sounds
inside his mind.

Somehow he gathers
all those fragments
into melody,
and he writes music.

I think it's magic
of the most creative kind.

In the evenings,
       while we still can,
    we walk our country roads.

We don't even wait
until the dishes
have been done.
They'll be there
when we come home,
unlike the autumn sun.

For every evening's
shorter now,
and sometimes
we're still walking home
when the sun is down.

Though we hurry
just a little,
we always feel
the effort is worthwhile.

For summer walks
are lovely,
but there's something
very special
about country roads
so quickly dark
when you're walking into fall.

Daffodills

Rainy days remind me
of when my son was small.
He always made it a rule
to step in every puddle
while walking home from school.

I can see him still,
in his little yellow slicker,
splashing slowly down the street,
where every single puddle
seemed a magnet for his feet.

It made me smile
to see him having so much fun...
the shiny yellow slicker
reflecting in each puddle
like a welcome shaft of sun.

It's just a little picture
that my heart has stored away.
But oh how well it brightens
a dreary, rainy day.

Mrs. *Vona's Dairy Mart,*
   Grandmother called her store.

And it was a point of pride with her
that people came clear from Uniontown
just for her hand-packed ice cream.

The sandwiches from her deli-case
were equally well-stuffed.

She was generous, too,
with her time.
She seldom closed the store,
even on holidays.

The truth was, she said,
she'd rather be there than anywhere,
and her customers felt the same way.

Times changed
and big markets arrived,
but Grandmother's store still thrived.

And right up until her very last days,
people still came
clear from Uniontown
just for her hand-packed ice cream.

"Come with me, Mom", he said.
"We'll ride our bikes
down to the beach
and I'll teach you
how to dig for clams."

But I just didn't have
the time.
Things had that worn,
neglected look,
and needed my attention.

Another day,
when I'd be more
caught up,
would have to do.

But now he's grown,
and so have I...
enough to know
I could have had the time.

Where I live
    I can see
miles and miles of sky.

I can see rain clouds
gathering dark
long before their shadows
cover my yard.

I can see storms
in the mountains
a county away,
while the sun still shines
on my porch.

And even as rain
pours off of my roof,
I can see slivers of sunlight
following far in the sky.

I like it that way.
It makes me aware
of my little place
in nature's powerful plan.

And proper perspective is easy,
when you live
where you see miles of sky.

Last year at Christmas,
        for the very first time,
    my daughter baked
            the traditional cookies
and holiday breads
        her grandmother always makes.

Recipes my mother learned
from her mother years ago.
Some written down on paper,
and some from memory...
filtered down
through different branches
of our family tree.

And as the aromas
filled the house
with memories of their flavor,
my daughter wisely noted
that teaching her those recipes
was one of the finest
Christmas gifts
her grandmother ever gave her.

On the workbench in our garage
is a large wooden tool box,
with a name hand lettered on it.
It belonged to my Father-in-law.

When he was eighty,
he came to live with us.
Most of his days were spent
working on his projects,
in the shop in our garage.
And he was often joined
by my husband and my son.

One year, as a present,
my husband built
that special tool box for his Dad,
and it became his father's pride.

Years later, when he left us,
his tool box stayed behind.
As he would have wanted,
its tools are still in use
by my husband and my son.

And of all the places in my house
where his memory still clings,
it calls to me the clearest
from the workbench in our garage.

She was the schoolteacher one.
    The aunt with bookshelves filled
with all the classics
        of history and literature.

She was the one who knew Latin,
and read Shakespeare
like others read the morning paper.

Her books were her prize possessions,
and she seldom let them stray
outside her room.

So it was an honor,
when we went to visit,
that I was allowed
to sit in her room and read.

While the rest of the family
visited downstairs,
I'd be reading those wonderful pages
that challenge the mind and heart.

I don't see her anymore.
We live too far apart.
But I hope she knows
she's one of the reasons why,
in our family,
I became the schoolteacher one.

It was the kittens' first day outside.
I watched them
so they wouldn't stray
too far away from home.

They'd been so anxious to go out,
their days inside
were mostly spent on the window sill.

As soon as I let them out the door,
they sniffed and scurried
and scampered everywhere.

I worried I would lose them,
but after just an hour,
they headed for the house
they'd been so glad to leave before.

Once back inside,
their window sill˙
had lost its great appeal.
They curled up close in their basket,
and exhausted, fell asleep.

Already, they'd discovered
what some of us never learn.
It's good to go adventuring,
but it's even better
to be able to come home.

You made it easy for me.
The many mistakes
I know I made,
you just seemed
to take in stride.

Eager to please,
and willing to wait,
you let me have
the time it takes
to get it right.

And there were days
I struggled so
with being a brand new mom.

But somehow you knew
if I could only learn on you,
I'd improve as I went along.

So you made it easy for me.
And earned my eternal gratitude,
my wise little
first born child.

My daughter wears
the bracelet now...
an elegant circle of gold,
with a delicate design
etched into the soft shine
of its polished surface.

Inside, a small inscription
signifies it as a gift
from a husband to his bride.

My grandmother wore it
for many years,
then gave it to my mother,
who passed it on to me.

Each of us, in turn,
instructed to enjoy it
and wear it often.
And each of us, in turn,
also taught to realize
gold is not the reason
the bracelet's prized.

Its greatest value lies
in its continued circle
of cherished family ties.

Sometimes in the quiet night,
when it's been awhile
* since I've seen my children,*
*   I think about the mare and foal.*

At a horse show once,
I saw a fine old mare,
standing quietly at the rail
with her rider on her back.

As each horse appeared in the arena,
the mare was calm and unconcerned.
Then one certain horse
entered the arena.
The mare was suddenly aware,
and cried out in recognition.

The other horses all stayed silent.
But the one in the arena
broke his stride
and answered back.

Later on I learned
they were mare and foal,
separated years ago
when her colt was sold.

And sometimes in the quiet night,
my heart still hears her cry.
Especially when it's been awhile
since I've seen my children.

For me,
the most logical solutions
are the emotional ones.
They are the ones
I can live with.

You can give me
all your profound reasons
why I should choose
a course of action
that is logically the best,
but if I must be the one
to make it work,
then I must first know
in my own mind,
that it's right.

And that knowledge
doesn't come from reason.
For me,
it must come from the heart.

We never used the front door
when we visited Aunt Jean's.

She had one, I remember,
but everyone...
neighbor children,
relatives and friends,
and even the family dog...
went in and out
her kitchen door.

She preferred it that way,
and so did we.
There was a nice familiarity
in the sound of her screen door.
Perhaps because we knew,
somewhere inside,
her warm welcome waited.

She's gone now,
from her kitchen.
But I know she'd have been pleased,
that when we talk about her,
each of us remembers
we never used the front door
when we visited Aunt Jean's.

*I was all dressed up and waiting
while the music played.*

But my high hopes for the evening
drifted by like all the dancers .
For time went on, and no one there
wished to dance with me.

Then my younger brother
asked me for a dance.
And as we moved around the floor,
I was so disappointed
that my brother
was the only one who asked me.

I thought it was an evening
I would try hard to forget.
But now I see
that summer night of many years ago,
with a brighter and a clearer
point of view.
It's an evening
I am happy to remember.

And the best part of the memory
is that my younger brother
asked me for a dance.

Twenty eight years ago,
  I had a son.

Like many mothers before me,
I was convinced
I had been given
a most magnificent gift
because this child was mine.

But now I know
the greater gift
is that he grew
from child to man,
and never gave me
any real cause
to ever change my mind.

I stood there
looking at the flowers
in the florists shop.

I admired each beautiful bouquet,
so artfully arranged.
But my mind was on
another small arrangement.
One made up of dandelions,
wispy weeds,
and fading little flowers
from a tolerant neighbor's yard.

They were hand delivered
at my kitchen door,
a long, long time ago.

And though the little hand
that held them
had bunched the flowers up,
I remember they were lovelier
than any of the flowers
in the florist's shop.

Some people love the spring,
but I'm an autumn child.

Born in October,
and married in October too;
for me, the good things
often happen in the fall.

My autumn years are rich,
filled with the confidence
that comes from traveling awhile,
long enough to realize
I'm on the right road after all.

Approaching winter
doesn't frighten me.
When I feel
the crisp, clean chill
and see those colors rich and red,
I simply slip a sweater on
and quicken my step just a bit.

There's still much
that must be done,
but I'm certain now
that I can do it.
This is my best time,
for I'm an autumn child.

I learned about mornings from him.

> To me, it always seemed
> that the dawn was cold and dim.
> When I woke up early,
> I only wished
> to close my eyes again.
>
> To him, even on gray days,
> dawn was bright and fresh,
> as first light filtered in.
>
> He had a way
> of welcoming the day
> that made it well worth
> getting up early
> just to spend it with him.
>
> And it wasn't long
> before I learned
> that making mornings lovely
> is mostly attitude.

Daisies

I'd complain about the mess they made
and send them scrambling
to pick up their toys
from the living room floor.

They'd do it,
then try to convince me
how silly it was to put things away
at the end of a day
when tomorrow
they'd be out again.

It's something about which
parents and children very seldom agree.

Yet once they're grown,
in their own homes,
those lessons in neatness well-learned,
they understand.

We, on the other hand,
learn lessons too.
How much more alive
is a house, for example,
with toys on the living room floor.

The wind from the southeast
always brings our rain.
It's a better forecast
than the weatherman's.

When we moved here,
I still checked
the evening paper
for signs of sun or rain.
And they teased me
about being from the city.

For out here,
sophisticated satellites
and TV weather scans
are pretty much ignored.

These ranchers have relied for years
on proven old predictions,
and their rate of accuracy
has made me do the same.

Though I know the paper
calls for several days of sun,
I smell that southeast breeze
that's just beginning.
Better get the hay in.
Tomorrow, it will rain!

You were my shadow
when you were small.
Everywhere I went,
you tagged along.

People told me
to leave you behind from time to time,
or you'd be too dependent on me.
But I knew they were wrong.

Each child is different, I had learned,
and some cling longer
to mothers or dads
before they strike out on their own.

So I never urged you to leave my side,
nor did I urge you to stay.
Somehow I sensed
we both would know
when the time was right for you to go.

And how happy I am
that I followed my heart,
and enjoyed you
when you were a child.

For it didn't take very long at all,
before my shadow was gone.

My *father saves*
  the scraps of wood
that someone else
    would throw away.

He takes great pride
in making things of value
from leftovers.

His was the generation
that wasted nothing.
That's how families were fed
with the little
that was earned.

They made their way
by learning to make do.
Things were too hard to come by
to just be thrown away.

My house is filled
with lovely things
his patient hands have made.
And all of them more special,
to my father, and to me,
because they're made
from what he saved.

He's absorbed in what he's reading,
and he doesn't know
I'm studying his face.

It's a face that only shows
some of its sixty years.
The youthful spirit
underneath
has softened signs of age.

It's a face that shows
the strength of character it takes
to be a family man.

It's a face I've seen
so many years
that I know its every trace
of pain and happiness.

And even after all those years,
or perhaps because of them,
my heart still welcomes what I see
when I'm studying his face.

Fireworks and flags
        and the Fourth of July
                bring a memory to mind...
    a boy of four,
        and one small town parade.

It was the kind of local celebration
that everyone was part of...
the high school band, the ladies clubs
and the Veterans of Foreign Wars.

Anyone who wished to,
with a patriotic costume,
could be part of the parade.
So we helped him make
a cardboard horse,
and he dressed as Paul Revere.

I see him still, so serious and small,
marching straight and proud.

Others may prefer
much more professional parades,
but I like best
those small town celebrations...
with local bands and ladies clubs,
and little boys of courage,
dressed up like Paul Revere.

The day that you were born,
I should have sensed
that you would be
so many things to me.

For even as a child,
you learned to see
inside of me,
and understand.

And as you've gone
from child to woman,
I've never known neglect.
Though busy
with your own affairs,
you seem to still
enjoy my company.

You've become the sister
that I never had,
and the friend I measure
other friendships by.

How fortunate the day
that you were born to me.

Sometimes even before the words
are out of my mouth,
        I know I will regret them.

Sometimes even before the pain
shows on your face,
I know I've hurt you
with words
I never should have said.

Sometimes I catch myself in time,
and keep inside those words
that well up from my fear
and my frustration.

But sometimes they just tumble out,
relieving nothing
and solving even less.

That's when I hope your memory
is shorter than my patience,
and I pray you will forget.

For I remember
well enough for both of us
every word I've ever said
that caused you pain,
and filled me with regret.

Driving home
the other day,
I saw her sign.
"Ranch for sale," it read,
"thirty acres, reasonable price."

This was a place
I knew a bit about...
things that wouldn't fit
on one small sign.

Those thirty acres
had provided food and shelter
for several generations
of her family.
But a worn and weathered barn,
and a house,
neither big nor small,
could never tell it all.

Now no new fields were planted,
and the fence
was falling over from the rains.

The swing set in the yard
had been unused
for quite a while,
and the only growing things
were her flowers.

Her family was gone,
and she alone remained,
with little reason left
to be living on a ranch.

But I thought about the sign,
and I knew
the words were wrong.
It should have said,
"Ranch for sale,
thirty acres...priceless."

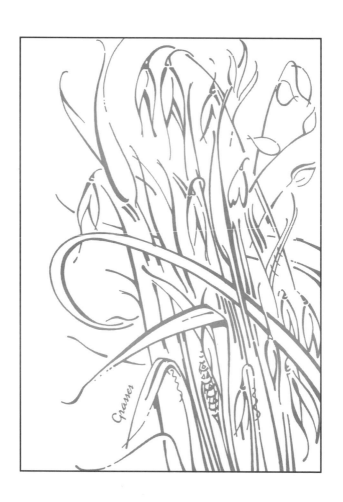

Grasses

Working into the sunset,
high atop his tractor,
red purple sky in front of him,
and dust billowing behind,
he pauses
and watches the sun go down.

Then the tractor lights come on
and he moves again,
into the long night.

With so much yet to do,
why did he stop
to watch the sunset?

Because he farms the land,
and though the work is hard,
it lets him be surrounded
with such a sense
of space and sky.

And a man may not be
good with words,
yet still have
the soul of a poet inside.

They took Cricket away yesterday.

Gentle bay mare,
struck down while still in her prime
by a rare form of pleurisy,
deadly to horses.

She was my daughter's horse.
No, she was more than that.

She was the dream a child saved up for,
four years of allowances
and birthdays and Christmas gift money
carefully put aside
until we finally found the mare...
waiting for the girl
who wanted a horse of her own
more than anything else in the world.

Cricket was the warm broad back
to lie down on, legs dangling,
talking with friends.
She was quiet rides up the hill

to watch the sunset,
but fast enough in field races
to make a young girl proud.

She was rain and mud
and hot, dusty days.
She was endless practice in the ring.
She was why we built the barn.

She was the part of my daughter's life
where all the hopes and dreams live.
She was ribbons won
and ribbons lost.
She was warm breath
and a welcoming murmur
on a damp, chilly morning.
She was life.

They took Cricket away yesterday.
And with her went a part of the child
who rode upon her back.

He's the uncle
who remembered their birthdays.

Work often kept him
far from home, and there were years
they seldom saw him,
but he always sent a gift
to my children on their birthdays.

Even when his work was lean,
and his life especially hard,
never once did he forget.

When they were small,
it was a present to be opened,
one they could count on to be there.

But when they were older,
less important was the present. . .
they began to value more
the consistent way he cared.
There grew a bond between them
of mutual affection,
and how that pleases me.

For they have learned
what I knew long ago.
Special is the man
who remembers children's birthdays.

Was there something
            you wanted to say?
   You paused in my doorway
            just now
as though you wished to talk,
            and then you turned away.

I was busy,
and my sense of urgency
must have led you to believe
I had no time for you today.

If you think that's true,
it's a sad situation.
For nothing I am doing
could ever keep me
from wanting to listen to you.

Now the moment's gone,
and I may never know
what you felt the need to say.
Please...the next time
you pause in my doorway...
stay.

Liquid Amber

Everywhere
we've ever lived,
he always planted trees.

He thinks that nothing
graces someone's home
like large and lovely trees.

But we've moved so often,
he seldom ever sees them
reach maturity.

And as the years go by,
he must surely realize
what he plants today
will only reach
their fine full size
when he is gone.

And what I've come
to most admire
is that he still plants trees.

Mrs. *Holden lived alone,*
in a big gray house,
two doors down.

Though I was only fifteen,
and she was a well-traveled widow
in her middle years,
we were fast friends.

I felt so "grown-up,"
drinking coffee
at her kitchen table
while she shared
her memories and philosophies.
She made me aware
of places and cultures
I had yet to see.

How proud I was
to know someone
of such sophistication.
And I used to wonder
if Mrs. Holden really knew
how much I valued
her friendship.

But now that I'm into
my own middle years,
I realize our relationship
might have meant
even more to her
than it did to me.

"They really change your life,
don't they?"
She said it with a smile,
and it was more a statement
than a question.

She was speaking
of her new firstborn,
amazed at all the changes
he was making in her world.

I nodded in agreement,
then she went on to say,
"I'm certain these adjustments
that I'm making now
will be the hardest ones."

It was now my turn to smile,
though I didn't say a word.
For nothing I could ever say
could quite convince her
that the changes in her life
were just beginning.

Adjustments that were harder still
would come to her one day,
when he grew up
and moved away.

The years
are showing up
on me.

I can see them
easily,
in every mirror
that I pass.

It's clear
with just a glance,
that I'm no longer
the girl I used to be.

Somehow
it doesn't bother me
the way I thought
it would.

Perhaps because
you never seem
to let it bother you.

She was cleaning out some closets,
and decided it was time
to throw some things away.
And then, she found the hat.

It was old,
and just a little crumpled,
but she gently placed it
on her head, and smiled.
She remembered how she felt
the first time that she wore it.

He had taken her
to meet his relatives.
Dressed up in her very best,
she put the hat on
as the final touch.

She wanted to impress them,
and make him proud.
And when she saw
his beaming smile,
she knew she had.

Carefully,
she placed the hat
back inside the closet,
and decided that it wasn't time
to throw some things away.

I *was shopping,*
    and I stopped
in a small restaurant
    to order some iced tea.

I looked around
and noticed
that the only one alone
was me.

I thought of all the times
we shopped together,
and stopped to sip
some coffee or some tea,
talking and laughing
with our packages
piled high.

And suddenly it seemed
shopping wasn't nearly
the fun it used to be.

I raised my glass
and silently saluted you
with a toast
no one could see.

In case, right then,
so many miles away,
you too had shopped,
and stopped,
and found yourself alone
like me.

My father always
spoke about his father
with such pride.

He told us often
how Grandpa came to this country
with only a strong back, a willing heart,
and an honest mind.

He dug coal,
and built grape arbors,
and anything else he could do
to keep his family here.

And when my Dad was old enough
he considered it an honor
to work alongside his father
laying miles of railroad track.

When Grandpa's health began to fail,
he had accomplished what he planned...
given each of his children
the opportunity to be an American.

And my father always
spoke about his father with such pride,
and said he was the finest man
he ever worked beside.

I would hear the hum of the tires
  on the highway,
 and my father's voice
    talking quietly to my mom,
  planning the trip as he drove.

My brother and I
would be all curled up,
sleepy and warm,
in the back of the old family car.

Outside the windows,
the stars would fly by
till the dark night
gave way to gray dawn.

That's how I remember
the start of each one
of those family trips
we took every summer of childhood.

And how sweet
the excitement I felt
at the sound of my father's voice
and the hum of the tires
on the highway.

One of the blessings
        of a good marriage
    is the shared silences.

Two people who are so in tune
with one another
that they can ride,
side by side in a car,
sometimes for an hour,
without the need for words.

Two people who can spend
an evening in the same room,
each doing something different
and seldom speaking,
yet satisfied completely
with each other's company.

They feel no need
to entertain or to impress.
They accept and they appreciate
the blessing
of shared silence.

If only growing up
came as easily
as growing old.

If all it took
to make us wise,
was just advancing years.

If the wrinkles and the gray hair
come to every one of us
unasked for,
and to most, unwelcome,
why couldn't wisdom also
be an automatic thing?

Ah, well, perhaps it is.

It just may be
we have acquired some wisdom
once we have learned
there's more to growing up
than growing old.

I remember the houses I've lived in,
not by street numbers
or size.
For me, they're identified
by my memories.

The first one was a cabin
where my small son played
in the tall wheat grass,
and I carried
my second child.

Another was the house
with the neighborhood playground
across the street,
and snowmen standing
in the front yard.

There was one
with model trains
in the loft
above the garage,
and a bedroom for Grampa,
filled with his favorite
old photographs.

Each one has its own
warm set of pictures
I keep in my mind.
And that's how I identify
the houses I've lived in.

It's been so full,
this life of mine,
I want it never to end.

Yet well I know,
like a river,
it follows its predestined path,
and nothing I do
can change its course
or alter the river's bend.

That's fine, I suppose,
for Heaven knows,
I've been a thousand times blessed.
It's only fair,
that after awhile,
I leave some space for the rest.

And one way I can accept that fact,
is just to know
that those I have loved
have loved me back.
And that knowledge may be
the best of the blessings
that fill this life of mine.

The second in a series, *When Wildflowers are in Bloom* is a collection of Rae Turnbull's heartwarming views of the everyday events that enrich each of our lives.

Rae is an author, teacher, and artist who lives on a small ranch in northern California with her husband, a retired Professor. Working in the upstairs office in their home, Rae devotes most mornings to her writing. Afternoons are spent teaching Art and Calligraphy at the local high school.

Rae's essays and short stories have appeared in such noted magazines as *First for Women* and *Good Housekeeping*. As a syndicated columnist, her poetic essays, with their reaffirmation of family values, have been a regular feature in several major newspapers in the west for over eight years.

The publication of her first book, *Echoes in the Corners of My Heart* in 1989, was a direct response to the many requests Rae received for just such a collection. Regular readers of Rae's work should recognize themselves in the very first essay of this book. It was written in their honor.